COVER TO COVER

BIBLE

7 SE

AND

G000299929

Elisha

A LESSON IN FAITHFULNESS

CWR

Christopher Brearley

Contents

Introduction

Great servants of God have a vision for the future and know when the time is right to step away from the work that He originally called them to. They recognise their own mortality, and the even more unpleasant fact of their unavoidable decline in strength of mind and body. Sometimes the transition of power from one leader to the next can be very difficult. Even so, good leaders do not attempt to stay in power way past their period of usefulness, when there are others who have been prepared by God to take their place. In the call of Elisha, we see the selfless character of Elijah. He willingly travelled northwards, through the Jordan valley, to Abel Meholah and anointed Elisha to be his successor. Elisha would go on to continue the fight against idolatry and restore the worship of the true God in the land of Israel.

We live in a period very similar to Elisha's, a period in which our belief in God is being severely challenged. Conditions of rampant secularism and an indifference towards the worship of the true and living God are far from encouraging. At times, it appears to many as if the work of God is finished. But that is a mistake because things are not always as they appear. God continues His work in every generation and it will end in triumph. It has been aptly said that God buries His workers but His work goes on. What a great encouragement this is!

Elisha, the son of Shaphat, appears on the stage of history in an abrupt way. We first see him ploughing a field with a team of oxen (1 Kings 19:19). He was industrious and practical, which is a good thing to see in any person. It is interesting to notice that God often chooses such people to do his work. For instance, when God called Moses, he was occupied with tending his father-in-law's flock (Exod. 3:1). David had cared for his father's sheep (1 Sam. 17:34–36). Jesus said to four fishermen, 'Come, follow me' (Matt. 4:18–22). The evangelist

D. L. Moody gave up selling shoes to save souls. Gladys Aylward, a parlour maid from London, effectively spread the message of Jesus in China. These were all hard-working people who God chose and it is the same now, in today's society. God takes ordinary people and by the power of His Spirit enables them to do extraordinary things.

As we explore the life of Elisha over the next seven weeks, through this study guide and the Leader's Notes at the back, it becomes clear that he was deeply concerned about the work of God. Hence, when the call of God came he did not hesitate to follow Elijah, despite the rigours and great hardship it would involve. He knew that his old life was finished and that a new life was about to begin in which he would be thoroughly devoted to serving his God. How do we respond to God's call? Obviously not everyone is called to leave their secular employment, but we are all called upon to serve according to our various abilities. What God requires is for each of us to sacrifice enough to fulfil the demands of our particular calling, without hesitation or reluctance.

Many of the works of Elisha replicate the work of Elijah. Even so, it is impossible not to notice the differences between these two prophets. They particularly have different approaches to working with other people. Elijah enjoyed a solitary existence whereas Elisha was much more sociable. He is often associated with a company of prophets (2 Kings 4:38–41; 6:1–7). Both prophets travelled extensively, but we know that Elisha had his own house in Samaria (2 Kings 6:32) and the use of a room in the town of Shunem (2 Kings 4:8–10). Elisha also had a personality that was far more gentle and gracious than that of Elijah. As a consequence, their ministries were very different. Elijah was primarily a stern messenger of judgment.. Elisha, on the other hand, was primarily a messenger of grace. His name meant 'God is salvation', and his parents most likely chose it as a profession of their personal faith.

Certainly, Elisha lived up to his name. The ministry of Elijah prepared people for Elisha's gracious message of reconciliation. Thus, Elijah was the Old Testament's version of John the Baptist (Matt. 11:14; 17:13) and Elisha's ministry can be likened to that of Christ.

The ministry of Elisha occupied more than half a century, during which he saw several kings reign and fall in Judea and Israel. In some ways, he was unique. He was called by God to minister at a particular time. Nevertheless, a careful study of his life provides an outstanding example for us all to follow. Elisha showed a great determination to receive what had been promised by the Lord and he would not be deterred by anyone (2 Kings 2:1–10). During his ministry he refused riches that were offered to him (2 Kings 5:15–16). His chief aim was always to do the will of God. Even on his deathbed, he emphasized the need of zeal for God. Elisha discovered how to walk closely with Him and, through faith, experience His power.

How closely do you walk with God currently? Do you rely on the power of the Holy Spirit to achieve what you could never achieve by yourself? Are you ready to discover what God teaches through His servant Elisha?

WEEK 1

Seize the Opportunity

Opening Icebreaker

When confronted with a challenge, often the most common and easiest reaction is to say, 'I will do it some other time.' Discuss why people might not seize an opportunity immediately, and to what extent is this true in your life?

Bible Readings

- 1 Kings 19:19–21
- 2 Kings 2:1–10
- Luke 9:57–62
- Matthew 4:18–22
- Luke 5:27–28

Opening Our Eyes

In accordance with the instructions he had received at Horeb, Elijah went to Abel Meholah to find Elisha, son of Shaphat. He found Elisha ploughing his father's field along with eleven other workers who were ahead of him. Without warning, Elijah went over to Elisha and, not saying a word, threw his cloak across the young man's shoulders and then walked away. Elisha immediately understood the significance of that act. He realized that Elijah was calling him to be his colleague and successor.

This call meant a major change for Elisha. He belonged to a family of considerable wealth. This is clear from the number of workers who were employed alongside him in ploughing the land. In the place of comfort he was now being offered a life of hardship, danger and great responsibility. It would also involve separation from his family and friends. Elisha was aware of the cost but, even though a degree of hesitation would be understandable, he seized the opportunity. He ran after Elijah and said to him, 'First let me go home and say goodbye to my father and mother, and then I will come with you.'

It appears that Elisha's farewells were speedily accomplished and that no objection was raised by his godly parents. He killed his oxen and used the wood from the plough to build a fire to roast their flesh for a celebratory meal. This showed that he was finished with his former life and fully committed to his new task. Elisha would go with Elijah and there would be no turning back.

A lengthy period of preparation was essential before Elisha was ready to take over. Thus, for several years he would serve Elijah as a personal attendant and perform many menial but necessary tasks. He became known as the one who 'used to pour water on the hands of Elijah' (2 Kings 3:11) – if you desire to exercise authority you must first learn to submit to it.

A time came when both Elijah and Elisha knew that their time together was drawing to a close (2 Kings 2:1–10). On their final journey, they travelled from Gilgal to Bethel, from Bethel to Jericho, and from Jericho to the River Jordan. At the beginning, and at each stop, Elijah suggested that he travel alone, but Elisha insisted on accompanying him every time. Elisha was determined to stay close to the man of God and to experience the many wonderful things in store for him.

On reaching the Jordan, Elijah divided the water with his folded cloak and the two of them went across on dry ground into the territory of Moab. Then the older prophet asked, 'Tell me, what can I do for you before I am taken away from you?' 'Let me inherit a double portion of your spirit,' Elisha replied (2 Kings 2:8). He did not want popularity, wealth or worldly power. Having served his apprenticeship, he wanted to be Elijah's rightful successor. Of course, only God could grant such a request.

The test would be whether or not Elisha had spiritual insight. His right to the succession is linked to his witnessing the departure of Elijah. It is at this point that the importance of his persistence is revealed. He stayed with his master until the end and saw all that happened. Then, when Elijah's cloak fell before him he knew that his request had been granted. How much this must have meant to him. To serve his God was something he wanted to do more than anything else.

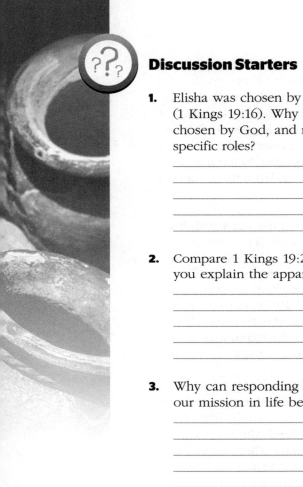

Discussion Starters

1. Elisha was chosen by God to succeed Elijah as prophet (1 Kings 19:16). Why is it essential that people are chosen by God, and not self-appointed, to fulfil specific roles?

2. Compare 1 Kings 19:20 with Luke 9:61–62. How do you explain the apparent contradiction?

3. Why can responding faithfully to God's call to fulfil our mission in life be very difficult?

4. It can sometimes seem as if we live in an age of insubstantial commitments. What should it mean to commit ourselves to God?

5. Elisha was determined to follow Elijah to the end, despite what anyone did or said (2 Kings 2:2–6). Why is endurance and perseverance so important for us?

_____

_____

_____

_____

_____

6. Character gives credibility. What characteristics should we expect to see in a Christian leader?

_____

_____

_____

_____

_____

7. Elisha performed many menial tasks for Elijah over a period of several years. Initially, this was even what he became known for. What do we learn from this?

_____

_____

_____

_____

_____

8. Christians are encouraged to serve others and set aside their selfishness (see Phil. 2:3–8). How does God respond to the humble?

_____

_____

_____

_____

_____

Personal Application

What does it mean to follow Jesus today? How do we respond to His call? Do we say, 'Lord, I will follow You but …?' Are we willing to be a disciple, but on our terms? The Gospels tell us of people who have tried to do this (Luke 9:57–62). However, there can be no excuses for half-heartedness. The first disciples of Jesus did not hesitate in abandoning their former way of life so that they might hear and obey His teachings. Such a personal relationship with Jesus can be just as real now as it was then. Remember, it's never too soon to follow Him, but at any moment it could be too late.

Seeing Jesus in the Scriptures

One day, as Jesus was walking beside the Sea of Galilee, He called two pairs of brothers, who were fishermen, to be His disciples. He first called Simon (also known as Peter), and Andrew. 'Come, follow me,' Jesus said, 'and I will send you out to fish for people' (Matt. 4:19). Even though they were busy at the time, casting a net into the lake, they seized their opportunity and followed Him. A little further up the shore, Jesus saw James and John, working in their father's boat. He called them to come too. Immediately, and without reservation, they followed Him (Matt. 4:21–22). Later, Jesus saw a tax collector named Levi (also known as Matthew) sitting at his tax booth. 'Follow me,' he told him, and Levi at once got up and left everything behind (Luke 5:27–28; Matt. 9:9). Following Jesus involves allegiance, commitment and change.

WEEK 2

Where is the Lord, the God of Elijah?

Opening Icebreaker

In today's society, tremendous emphasis is often placed on speed, how quickly things can be achieved. Some people achieve great success in this area, while others fail to keep up with the accelerating pace of life. Identify what you consider to be the necessary qualities to cope with pressure and responsibility, is speed one of them?

Bible Readings

- 2 Kings 2:11–18
- John 14:12–14
- 2 Timothy 4:6–8

Opening Our Eyes

As Elijah and Elisha were walking along, suddenly a chariot of fire appeared, drawn by horses of fire. It drove between them, separating them, and Elijah was taken by a whirlwind into heaven. Elisha saw him no more. All that remained was Elijah's cloak that had fallen from him as he ascended into heaven. So, with Elijah gone, how would Elisha respond to such great pressure and responsibility? He could pick up Elijah's cloak, or he could go his own way.

When Elijah disappeared from sight, Elisha took hold of his own clothes and tore them apart as a sign of personal mourning and public loss. But he was not defeated or even despondent. Immediately he picked up Elijah's fallen cloak, knowing that his time to lead had arrived. What was he to do next? Elisha believed that all good leaders showed courage because of their assurance of God's presence. Previously, he had asked for a double portion of Elijah's spirit and now his chance had arrived to see if he had received it. Could he, by means of the inherited cloak, repeat the last miracle performed by Elijah? We are not aware that Elisha had ever performed a miracle before.

Elisha knew that there was nothing magical about the cloak. Neither did he believe that his success was dependent upon Elijah. Hence, he does not ask 'Where is Elijah?' Instead he says, 'Where now is the LORD, the God of Elijah?' (2 Kings 2:14). This was not a cry of unbelief or doubt. It was a clear acknowledgement of his total dependence upon God, who had empowered his predecessor. Elijah had gone, but Elijah's God remained.

Courageously, Elisha took the cloak to the bank of the river and struck the water with it. On the other side of the river, prophets carefully witnessed this momentous event. Upon seeing the water part for Elisha, they accepted that he was truly qualified to be their leader: 'The spirit of Elijah is resting on Elisha' (2 Kings 2:15). They went to meet him and bowed down before him.

Nevertheless, despite this act, the prophets still wanted to search for Elijah. At first, Elisha advised them against such an action, as he knew that it was a waste of time. But, because of their persistence, he eventually told them to go. So, fifty men searched for Elijah for three days but, just as Elisha had said, they did not find him.

The acceptance of any new leader can be difficult. Some people make the mistake of trying to live in the past. They yearn for leaders who are no longer with them. How should we respond to change? This is a recurring challenge as people die or move to other locations. However, God is in the business of change. He remains the same forever, and He is able to help us as He helped His great servants in the past.

Where is the God of Elijah today? Where is the God of Isaiah, of Jeremiah, of Daniel, Paul and Peter? Where is the God of Wesley and of Spurgeon? Where is the God of the people who are no longer with us? Well, their God is our God too. Where then, we must ask, can He be found? The answer is that God is wherever someone acts in faith. The same Holy Spirit enables the children of God in every generation to do infinitely more than they could ever ask or imagine.

Discussion Starters

1. Remember, God does something different in each generation. People come and then, after a relatively short period, are replaced by successors. How should we react to change?

   _____

   _____

   _____

   _____

   _____

2. If we are consistently talking about what we did yesterday, perhaps we haven't done much today. Is it unhealthy for us to live in the past? Think about any examples from your own experience.

   _____

   _____

   _____

   _____

   _____

3. Is it significant that Elisha's first miracle should echo Elijah's last?

   _____

   _____

   _____

   _____

   _____

4. Why was Elisha recognised by the prophets as their new leader? How do we recognise leaders today?

   _____

   _____

   _____

   _____

   _____

5. The prophets begged Elisha to allow them to send fifty of their strongest men to search for Elijah. What do we learn from this?

_____

_____

_____

_____

_____

6. Why did Elisha advise the prophets not to search for Elijah?

_____

_____

_____

_____

7. Elisha eventually withdrew his opposition and told the prophets to search for Elijah. Was this a wise decision?

_____

_____

_____

_____

8. The God of Elijah and Elisha is also our God. He is the same yesterday, today, and forever. How should this affect the way we live?

_____

_____

_____

_____

Personal Application

Elisha has lost Elijah and reveals genuine grief (2 Kings 2:12). Similarly, there are times in our own lives when we grieve the loss of someone important to us. We grieve when we see loved ones suffer. Sometimes we may feel all alone, comforted by no one (Psa. 69:20; 2 Tim. 4:16). Where, then, is the only source of true comfort for us?

The Bible reveals that grief has its own season, but it is then necessary to move on to another (Eccl. 3:4). How can we turn our sadness into joy? Elisha knew that human effort by itself could not enable him to face the great tasks that lay ahead. He was also aware that he had not lost Elijah's God. Neither have we! God is still the same and His power is undiminished in every generation. He is the God who promises to be close beside us, forever.

Seeing Jesus in the Scriptures

Jesus did marvellous things whilst on earth, but now He is in heaven. How do we react to His departure? Let us take courage in the fact that anyone who has faith in Jesus will not experience a loss of power to do His work. We can ask for anything in His name, and He will do it, because the work of the Son brings glory to the Father (John 14:12–14). But, remember, such prayer, if it is to be successful, must always accord with God's will (Matt. 6:10; 1 John 5:14–15).

WEEK 3

Miracles

Opening Icebreaker

All God's people will, at some point in their lives, face discouragement. Discuss why you believe people get discouraged. Identify ways in which we can cope with discouragement.

Bible Readings
- 2 Kings 2:19–22
- 2 Kings 4:1–7, 38–44
- 2 Kings 6:1–7

Opening Our Eyes

It is very easy to read parts of the Bible and reach the
conclusion that miracles were a common occurrence.
That would be a mistake. By definition, miracles are rare,
even in biblical times. Conventionally, they are associated
with specific, relatively short periods, such as the time
of Moses and Joshua, during the ministries of Elijah and
Elisha, and when Jesus ministered with His early disciples.
Miracles do appear elsewhere in the Bible but they are few
and far between. A miracle would not be a miracle if it was
an everyday event.

The word 'miracle' can mean different things to different
people. But for a person who believes in God, it can simply
be defined as a natural event reacting in an unnatural way,
because of a supernatural influence. This pattern is applicable
to all miracles. Let us take the story of Elisha and his casting
of salt into polluted water to make it wholesome as an
example (2 Kings 2:19–22). This was a natural event in that
it was ordinary salt. It was an unnatural event in that salt
would not normally have made the water wholesome. The
reason for the purification was supernatural intervention. God
made it happen and Elisha acknowledged this: 'This is what
the LORD says: "I have healed this water. Never again will it
cause death or make the land unproductive"' (v21).

In 2 Kings 4, there are several signs of God's provision.
On one occasion, there is a woman in desperate need but
who knew where to seek help (2 Kings 4:1–7). Elisha tells
her to do something that requires faith. She has to ask all
her neighbours for lots of empty jars and bring them to her
home. Then, in private, she is to use the little oil she already
possesses to fill these jars. Miraculously, the oil flowed until
every jar was filled to the brim! This oil is then sold so that
she can pay her debts and provide for herself and her sons.

On another occasion, during a time of famine, Elisha instructs his servant to cook a meal for some hungry prophets. One of them went scavenging in the countryside and brought back some gourds. Although no one knew what they were, they were added to the stew. As the prophets began to eat their meal they became aware that there was 'death in the pot' (2 Kings 4:38–40), but Elisha put flour in the pot and said, 'Serve it to the people to eat' (v41). This would be a sign of their faith and of God's faithfulness towards them.

During this time of famine, there was another miracle. A man came to Elisha with twenty loaves and some new grain. It was clearly insufficient to feed all the people but, because of miraculous multiplication, they all ate and had some left over (2 Kings 4:42–44). As a miracle, it can be compared to the later feeding of the five thousand by Jesus (Matt. 14:13–21).

Some miracles, such as the floating iron axe-head, can appear to be trivial and maybe bizarre (2 Kings 6:1–7). This miracle, however, is not only a demonstration of God's power but also of His providential care. God can recover what is lost. We can ask God to help us to find lost things, whether they are spiritual or physical. Our problems are important to God, even very small ones (Phil. 4:6). To believe in a God of miracles means that we can rely on His power, protection and provision for our greatest needs.

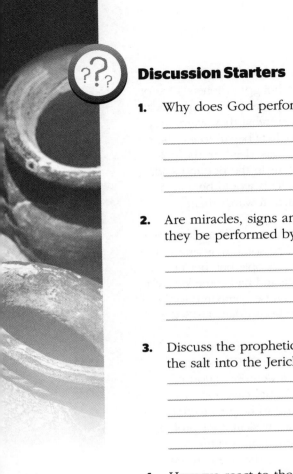

Discussion Starters

1. Why does God perform miracles?

_____
_____
_____
_____
_____

2. Are miracles, signs and wonders all from God, or can they be performed by others?

_____
_____
_____
_____
_____

3. Discuss the prophetic significance of the casting of the salt into the Jericho spring (2 Kings 2:19–22)?

_____
_____
_____
_____
_____

4. How we react to the circumstances of life, whether pleasant or painful, is tremendously revealing. Do you, like Elisha, remain faithful whatever the circumstances? What are the rewards of faithfulness?

_____
_____
_____
_____
_____

5. Consider the parallels between the widow at Zarephath (1 Kings 17:1–16) and the widow in 2 Kings 4:1–7.

_____

_____

_____

_____

_____

6. 2 Kings 4:1–7 tells the story of a widow whose husband had died, leaving her with the problem of unpaid debts. Furthermore, the creditor was threatening to take her two sons into slavery in order to pay the debts. How did she react? What does it mean to trust God's provision?

_____

_____

_____

_____

_____

7. 2 Kings 6:1–7 teaches us more than the restoration of the lost axe-head. What lessons are there for us to learn from this?

_____

_____

_____

_____

_____

8. Do miracles still occur today? Have you experienced any personally?

_____

_____

_____

Personal Application

Elisha was enabled by God to perform more miracles than any other prophet in the Old Testament. Other great servants of God had very different ministries. Abraham and David, as far as we know, never performed a miracle. John the Baptist also didn't complete any miracles, and yet Jesus testified that up to the days before He came, there was none greater than John (Matt. 11:11). Nevertheless, our God is a God of miracles and will intervene when He has a good reason to do so. At the same time, we should remember that the Bible is an adequate record of our need to believe in God's greatest miracle – the new birth that He has promised to all who believe in the Lord Jesus Christ.

Seeing Jesus in the Scriptures

Many people exclaim, 'if only God would perform a miracle, a sign or a wonder, then I would believe in Him!' But the Bible reveals that this is not necessarily so. Numerous people witnessed the many impressive miracles of Jesus. Yet, irrespective of all that He did, the great majority still would not believe in Him (John 12:37).

If Jesus performed the same miracles today as He did in the past, people would still reject Him. It is wrong to seek miraculous signs to satisfy curiosity or to substantiate the claims of Jesus (see Luke 23:8). Saving faith is never based upon physical senses but instead upon the inner conviction of the Holy Spirit (John 16:8). That is why the miracle accounts of Jesus often reveal that while some people believed in Him, others did not.

WEEK 4

Miraculous Healing

Opening Icebreaker

It has been suggested that if people are healthy and wealthy they will be happy. But how wrong this is! Consider why health and wealth by themselves do not lead to true happiness.

Bible Readings

- 2 Kings 5:1–19
- Luke 4:25–27
- John 9:1–3

Opening Our Eyes

One of the most familiar Old Testament examples of miraculous healing is that of Naaman. He was commander of the army of Aram (Syria) and had a fine reputation as a victorious leader. The king had high admiration for him, but, despite all of his achievements, he was a man in great need. He suffered from leprosy. Naaman was someone who had almost everything except a worthwhile future.

A young girl was taken from Israel by Aramean fighters and given to Naaman's wife as a maid. It's difficult to imagine this girl's sense of loss as she was forcibly removed from her family and friends to a foreign land. Nevertheless, she was not bitter or resentful. This girl expressed a genuine love for people and continued to believe in God. Furthermore, she knew that Elisha was God's prophet and that he could heal Naaman of his leprosy, so she took the opportunity of testifying for her God.

The girl's age, nationality and position in society were all against her. Even so, Naaman listened to what she had to say and went to Israel. In preparation for his journey, he obtained wholehearted support of the king of Aram and also arranged to take valuable gifts with him. However, he soon realised that you cannot buy blessings from God.

The king of Israel could not help Naaman and did not know where to turn for an answer until Elisha intervened. 'Make the man come to me and he will know that there is a prophet in Israel' (2 Kings 5:8). So Naaman went with his horses and chariots to Elisha's house, but on his arrival he received a shock. Elisha did not even go to the door to meet him. Instead, a messenger was sent with a very simple solution. Naaman was to go and wash himself seven times in the River Jordan, if he did that he would be healed. Naaman had expected something different. He had his own idea of what needed to be done, so he went away in a rage.

At this point Naaman's loyal servants respectfully reminded him of the need for humility. He listened to their advice and obeyed Elisha's command, and, as promised, he was instantly cleansed from his leprosy. A grateful Naaman returned to Elisha with his entourage to give thanks. He openly declared his newfound faith in God and urged the prophet to accept gifts. This was not because he thought he could purchase anything from God; rather it was because he desired to show thankfulness. Elisha refused to accept any reward for his work, which contrasted with the attitude of false prophets and of Gehazi at the time (2 Kings 5:20–24).

Naaman then made two requests. Firstly, he asked if he can take some of Israel's soil back home. Secondly, he asked whether the prophet would understand that he must still attend the temples of other gods. Evidently, Naaman was superstitious and lacked commitment. His knowledge of God was still weak, but his concern about the problems he would face is clear proof of the genuineness of his conversion. 'Go in peace' Elisha said as Naaman departed (2 Kings 5:19).

Discussion Starters

1. How does the reaction of the young girl (2 Kings 5:3) differ from that of the king of Israel (v7)? What major lessons do we learn from each of them?

    _____
    _____
    _____
    _____
    _____

2. Naaman arrived at Elisha's house and left in a rage (2 Kings 5:11–12). Why was this?

    _____
    _____
    _____
    _____
    _____

3. Why did Elisha refuse to accept Naaman's gifts (2 Kings 5:15)?

    _____
    _____
    _____
    _____
    _____

4. How do you explain Naaman's request to take back home two loads of soil from Israel (2 Kings 5:17)?

    _____
    _____
    _____
    _____
    _____

5. Naaman believes in the God of Israel. He does, however, ask forgiveness for when he enters the temple of Rimmon as part of his duty to the king of Aram. Does this suggest that he lacks total commitment?

_____

_____

_____

_____

_____

6. What parallels can you identify between Naaman's leprosy and our situation as sinners?

_____

_____

_____

_____

7. Read 2 Kings 5:19–27. Why did Gehazi do what he did?

_____

_____

_____

_____

8. When Gehazi left Elisha's presence he was leprous, as white as snow (v27). Consider whether sickness is related to personal sin; what do you think and why?

_____

_____

_____

_____

Personal Application

It is possible to become disillusioned by modern claims of miraculous healing. It often appears to be based on sensationalism and not corroborated by sound evidence. In biblical times, healings were clearly miraculous. For example, those suffering from skin diseases, blindness or paralysis were completely and instantaneously healed without any known instance of relapse. Most Christian healings that we hear about today are very different to these. That is not to say that they are false. If we are sick, we should pray about it, knowing that God has the power to heal any affliction. We need, however, to remember that God sometimes chooses not to heal (2 Cor. 12:7–9). Whatever the outcome, we need not fear! Anything God's people suffer in this world will be nothing compared with the glory in the next (2 Cor. 4:17).

Seeing Jesus in the Scriptures

Jesus, whilst speaking in the synagogue at Nazareth, gave two Old Testament illustrations of Jews rejecting genuine prophets (Luke 4:22–27). Firstly, Elijah was helped by a widow from Zarephath in Sidon, not by Jews (compare vv25–26 with 1 Kings 17:8–24). Secondly, Elisha healed Naaman, a Syrian, rather than the many lepers in Israel who needed help (compare v27 with 2 Kings 5:1–14). Does this suggest that God was not interested in Israelite widows or Israelite lepers? Of course not! Whoever believes, regardless of their nationality or status, will not be turned away. The people of Nazareth met Jesus and drove him out. He could only do a few miracles there because of their unbelief (Matt. 13:58).

WEEK 5

Divine Guidance

Opening Icebreaker

Read Psalm 23 together. Consider the various ways in which a person can experience God's guidance. How is this relevant to you?

Bible Readings

- 2 Kings 3:1–27
- 2 Kings 6:24–7:20

Opening Our Eyes

As told in 2 Kings 3, the attempt by the kings of Israel, Judah and Edom to quash the rebellion of Mesha of Moab teaches us some important lessons. For instance, the route they took to attack Moab was wrong. After seven days of travelling through the wilderness they had no water. Death seemed inevitable. It was then that they decided to consult God. If they had done so and honoured Him at the outset they would not have been in this desperate situation.

Elisha was nearby and the three kings went to him. It was, however, for Jehoshaphat king of Judah alone that Elisha was prepared to deliver the others from disaster. Relaxed by the playing of a harpist, Elisha received two messages from God. The first was that ditches must be dug and then, without wind or rain, they would be filled with water. The second was that they will be victorious over Moab.

Early next morning the Moabites saw the water but, because of the rising sun, it appeared like blood on the ground. 'It's blood!' the Moabites said. 'The three armies have fought among themselves and killed each other! Let's go and collect the plunder!' So they rushed into the Israelite camp and were slaughtered.

Later we read about how the siege of Samaria caused distress, which was followed by deliverance and delight (2 Kings 6:24–7:20). There was a famine and so the people were driven to eat whatever they could get. Some of the city's inhabitants even resorted to cannibalism. In such extreme circumstances, it is usual to look for someone to blame. Hence, Israel's king vows to destroy God's prophet, Elisha. He had also decided to no longer wait upon God, but to surrender to Ben-Hadad.

As on previous occasions, Elisha had supernatural knowledge. He knew what the king intended to do to him but he remained calm and confident. He knew precisely what would happen, by the next day the price of basic commodities would fall well below the normal price. Elisha did not say how this would be achieved. The officer assisting the king said that it was impossible. Elisha's reply was serious. He told the scoffer that his eyes would see it happen, but that he would not benefit from any of it.

Elisha's prophecy was fulfilled. The Lord caused the whole army of Aram to hear the sounds of a great army approaching. 'The king of Israel has hired the Hittite and Egyptian kings to attack us!' they cried (2 Kings 7:6). Thus, they fled in complete confusion, abandoning most of their possessions.

The first to discover what had happened were four lepers. These men had nothing to lose and possibly something to gain. So they went to the camp of the Arameans and find abundant food, clothing and wealth. Then they realised their obligation to share this good news with others who were starving. Hence, they went to Samaria. The king suspected a trick and was fearful to act. Nevertheless, scouts were sent who confirmed Elisha's prophecy of provision. The prophecy of judgment was also fulfilled (2 Kings 7:18–20).

What Elisha said was not vague speculation. He was even able to reveal to the king of Israel the private thoughts of the king of Aram (2 Kings 6:12). Repeatedly, during his ministry, Elisha's prophecies were accurate to the letter. If Israel had listened to him, things would have been very different. Now, as then, if we obey God's Word, the Bible, it will transform our lives.

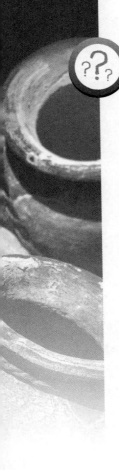

Discussion Starters

1. The kings of Israel, Judah and Edom formed a coalition to fight against the king of Moab (2 Kings 3:4–9). What is wrong with this?

   _____
   _____
   _____
   _____
   _____

2. Are there alliances that can cause Christians to compromise? Consider 2 Corinthians 6:14–15.

   _____
   _____
   _____
   _____
   _____

3. Elisha only cooperates because of the presence of Jehoshaphat king of Judah (2 Kings 3:14). Why was this?

   _____
   _____
   _____
   _____
   _____

4. Why is discerning God's will essential?

   _____
   _____
   _____
   _____
   _____

5. Did the king show any signs of true repentance (2 Kings 6:30)? How do you know?

_____

_____

_____

_____

_____

6. The king of Israel wanted to kill Elisha (2 Kings 6:31). What are his reasons?

_____

_____

_____

_____

_____

7. What important lessons relating to the gospel message can we learn from 2 Kings 7:1–20?

_____

_____

_____

_____

_____

8. There was a man who saw what happened, but was not able to enjoy the benefits of it (2 Kings 7:19–20). What do you understand by this?

_____

_____

_____

_____

_____

Personal Application

God guides His people. For instance, Abraham was told to leave his country, his friends, and go to another land (Gen. 12:1). Observe that God did not immediately tell him where that land was. He must step out in faith and rely on God to guide him to a final destination. God told Elijah to go and anoint Elisha (1 Kings 19:16). He directed Philip to the Ethiopian eunuch (Acts 8:26–29) and Paul was called to Macedonia (Acts 16:6–10).

God constantly calls people today to follow Him and take the Bible as their guide. His Word will be a lamp for their feet and a light for their path (Psa. 119:105).

Seeing Jesus in the Scriptures

Jesus made it clear that, in life, there are wide and narrow gates, and broad and narrow roads (Matt. 7:13, 14). By this He undoubtedly draws the routes of obedience and disobedience to our attention. The first of these is narrow and the gate is small because it is the way of self-denial and service. In contrast, the highway to hell is broad and its gate is wide. It is the way of selfishness and self-righteousness. The mass of humanity follow this easy way that leads to destruction. Only the few ever find the gateway to abundant life God has prepared for them.

Does entrance through the narrow gate mean that the route will be straightforward? Not at all! Christians need to constantly keep their eyes fixed upon Jesus so as to guard against those who can lead them astray.

WEEK 6

Divine Protection

Opening Icebreaker

It is sometimes said that the best way to conquer an enemy is with the weapon of love. Do you consider this to be wise advice? Give reasons for your decision.

Bible Readings

- 2 Kings 2:23–24
- 2 Kings 6:8–23
- Matthew 5:43–48
- Galatians 6:7–8

Opening Our Eyes

Whilst Elisha was walking along the road towards Bethel, some youths who had come from there began mocking and making fun of him. He responded by cursing them in the name of the Lord. 'Then two bears came out of the woods and mauled forty-two of the youths' (2 Kings 2:24, NIV 1984). This incident would appear, at first sight, to bring no credit to either Elisha or his God. Isn't it a vicious overreaction to an offensive group of children? In order to answer that question we must consider certain facts.

Firstly, these were probably not 'children' as we would understand it. The Hebrew word that describes them can cover a range of ages from infant to young adult. Whatever their age it would appear that the attack was premeditated. Secondly, it was not just youthful ridicule. They are hostile towards God's newly appointed prophet and aimed to curtail his ministry.

Elisha did not tell God what to do. He simply asked God to deal with the situation, and God acted. The youths were mauled by two bears, but did they die? The Bible is not specific regarding their fate. What is certain is that people learned a lesson that day and it would not be forgotten. God treats people according to how they treat His servants, and ultimately how they treat Him.

Another episode in Elisha's life takes us to Dothan. He awakes one morning to find himself surrounded by Aramean soldiers who had come to kidnap him. His servant was terrified by such powerful opposition and wondered what they could do. Elisha, however, remained calm and confident. He knew that the angelic army of the living God protected him. There was no way anyone could capture Elisha. Nevertheless, his servant was not convinced, so Elisha prays for him, and his eyes are opened to see 'the hills full of horses and chariots of fire all round Elisha' (2 Kings 6:17).

As the Aramean army advanced towards them, Elisha used the weapon of prayer. He prayed that his enemies would not be able to either recognise him or know his whereabouts. Notice that he did not pray for their destruction. Rather, he led them to Samaria, which was an Israelite stronghold. Here Elisha was safe, whereas the Aramean army were in grave danger. No doubt, when their sight was restored to normality, it would appear to be a hopeless situation. They had walked into a trap and were now totally dependent upon the mercy of their enemy. The king of Israel was ready to kill them, but Elisha's response was to spare them. Elisha knew that it was the Lord who had captured the Aramean army and it was His prerogative alone to decide their fate. So the king prepared a feast for them and then sent them back home.

Some people believe that the Old Testament is about killing and revenge whilst the New Testament is about love and forgiveness. But such an assumption is false. Justice and mercy occur throughout the Bible, and that is what we should expect, because it is all the Word of God. 2 Kings 6:20–23 is a wonderful example of love and forgiveness. The king of Israel would have killed the trapped Arameans, but he was told by Elisha to treat them kindly. There are two main ways to deal with enemies, you can either kill them or try to make them a friend. Let us not forget that Jesus instructs us to love our enemies (Matt. 5:44).

Discussion Starters

1. The youths jeered Elisha. 'Get out of here, baldy!' they said (2 Kings 2:23). How would you answer someone who suggested that this was harmless fun and that Elisha overreacted?

_____

_____

_____

_____

_____

2. Why did Elisha receive such a hostile reception from the people of Bethel?

_____

_____

_____

_____

3. Should all God's servants expect to encounter opposition? Are there any episodes in your life where you have been surprised, one way or another?

_____

_____

_____

_____

_____

4. The apostle Paul wrote, 'We are hard pressed on every side, but not crushed; perplexed, but not in despair; persecuted, but not abandoned; struck down, but not destroyed' (2 Cor. 4:8–9). How can God's servants overcome personal abuse?

_____

_____

_____

_____

5. If God is for us, it matters not who is against us. Why is this?

_____

_____

_____

_____

_____

6. Does God treat people according to the way that they treat others?

_____

_____

_____

_____

_____

7. Think of some biblical examples of angelic intervention.

_____

_____

_____

_____

_____

8. Are the angels that helped Elisha also available to help us? Give reasons for your answer.

_____

_____

_____

_____

_____

Personal Application

Faithful Christians will often feel like social misfits in a sinful world. In such a world, persecution, in one form or another, is inevitable. How then should we respond? We could easily become overwhelmed by the forces massed against us and echo the cry of Elisha's servant: 'Oh no, my lord! What shall we do?'. At such times, a proper perspective is essential. Instead of looking negatively at our problems, Christians must look positively to the future and realise that our present sufferings are temporal, but the glory to follow is never-ending. Then, like Paul, we can say, 'I consider that our present sufferings are not worth comparing with the glory that will be revealed in us' (Rom. 8:18).

Seeing Jesus in the Scriptures

A lawyer once asked Jesus a question that many others before him had debated, 'Teacher, which is the greatest commandment in the Law?' Jesus replied: '"Love the Lord your God with all your heart and with all your soul and with all your mind." This is the first and greatest commandment. And the second is like it: "Love your neighbour as yourself"' (Matt. 22:36–39). Jesus even went so far as to say, 'Love your enemies and pray for those who persecute you' (Matt. 5:44). Jesus Christ was a living example of unfailing love, even to death (Luke 23:34). Being a Christian requires that we love others (John 13:34–35), and that is proof that we belong to Christ. True love, like that of Christ, is always willing to treat our persecutors with kindness rather than bitterness.

WEEK 7

A Ministry Fulfilled

Opening Icebreaker

Christians believe that God has a plan for our lives. Discuss how we might discover what this is.

Bible Readings

- 2 Kings 8:1–15
- 2 Kings 9:1–13
- 2 Kings 13:14–21

Opening Our Eyes

In our final study, this week we shall consider five important incidents. We first read about a woman from Shunem returning home (2 Kings 8:1–6). Previously, she had shown great kindness to Elisha and in return he had prayed for her to have a son. When the son died, Elisha had prayed for him to be restored to life (2 Kings 4:8–37). Later he told her to move from her land because there would be a seven-year famine in Israel. She did as he said and took her family to live in the land of the Philistines for seven years. Then she returned to Israel to reclaim her property and, because of divinely planned intervention, everything was eventually restored to her. This woman's life clearly reveals how God provides for His people again and again.

Following this, we are told about how God used a wicked man to fulfil His purpose (2 Kings 8:7–15). God had said to Elijah that Hazael would become king of Aram (1 Kings 19:15–17). Elisha knew that Hazael would murder the present king, Ben-Hadad, and also that he would do terrible things to the people of Israel. This would be God's judgment on His own people, and it caused Elisha to weep. He realised that Hazael would become one of the most formidable threats to Israel during his forty-year reign in Damascus. In due course, however, the Arameans would be punished because of their cruelty (Amos 1:3–4). This punishment would impress upon people the seriousness of sin.

Our next character is Jehu, a member of Ahab's bodyguard, who was anointed king over Israel (2 Kings 9:1–13). The fact that Jehu was anointed by God does not mean that he was a godly man. Quite the contrary! He was a very violent man. Yet God used his wickedness as a means of bringing to an end the ungodly line of Omri that had lasted for four generations. Although God is slow to anger and abounding in love, the ultimate penalty of all sin is death (Rom. 6:23).

After a ministry of almost sixty years, we come to the closing events of Elisha's life. As he lay dying, King Jehoash of Israel visited him and wept over him. "'My father! My father!" he cried. "The chariots and horsemen of Israel!'" (2 Kings 13:14, they are words Elisha himself used when Elijah was taken away by God – see 2 Kings 2:12). Elisha was obviously highly thought of by the king. But the king's major concern was not the result of godliness; rather it was a fear that God's protection over the people would be removed. Hence, Elisha's last prophecy was to emphasise the necessity of zeal for God. Much to the annoyance of Elisha, the king held back from full commitment.

Elisha eventually died, but that was not the end. In 2 Kings 13:20–21, we read about a dead body being hurriedly thrown into the tomb of Elisha. Immediately as it landed on Elisha's bones, the dead man revived and jumped to his feet! This amazing incident is a continuation of the prophet's ministry to Israel. It served as a reminder to them to believe in his prophecies and also to remember that though he was no longer with them, the God of Elisha still lived. God is eternal. His presence, power and provision are available to all those who seek Him and act in faith.

Discussion Starters

1. Read 2 Kings 8:4–5. Has Gehazi been cured of his leprosy? Or is it conceivable that the king might converse with a leper? Why do you think this?

    _____
    _____
    _____
    _____
    _____

2. The woman from Shunem did as the man of God instructed (2 Kings 8:2). What does God promise to those who obey Him?

    _____
    _____
    _____
    _____
    _____

3. Why should Ben-Hadad consult Elisha (2 Kings 8:8), rather than the priests at the temple of Rimmon where he regularly worshipped?

    _____
    _____
    _____
    _____
    _____

4. What important lessons do we learn from the life of Hazael?

    _____
    _____
    _____
    _____
    _____

5. Think of some biblical examples of God using people who appear to be wicked for the accomplishment of His purposes.

_____

_____

_____

_____

_____

6. Why did Elisha rebuke Jehoash (2 Kings 13:19)?

_____

_____

_____

_____

7. Seemingly, Elisha didn't stop performing miracles, even when he had died (2 Kings 13:20–21)! What is the significance of this amazing incident and what does it tell us about the power of God?

_____

_____

_____

_____

_____

8. As we come to the conclusion of our study, what important lessons have you learnt from the life of Elisha?

_____

_____

_____

_____

Personal Application

What a 'coincidence' that the woman from Shunem met Elisha, as he happened to travel her way. Later, she and her son arrived in Samaria at the precise moment that Gehazi was talking about them to the king. As a result, the property that had been taken from her was restored with interest. How 'lucky' she was! No, these were in fact acts of providence, maybe answers to prayer, of how God cares for His people. With God, things don't just happen, everything is planned. Consequently, there are no such things as chance or luck.

Seeing Jesus in the Scriptures

Prophetic vision enabled Elisha to see the terrible things that would happen to the people of Israel when Hazael becomes king of Aram. He will burn their fortified cities, kill their young men, dash their children to the ground, and rip open their pregnant women (2 Kings 8:12). This was God's judgment upon His own people, and these scenes of horror unsurprisingly caused Elisha such distress that he wept.

As Jesus approached Jerusalem and saw the city ahead, He began to weep (Luke 19:41). The crowd thought it was a day of triumph, but He saw it as a day of tragedy. Jesus knew the suffering that would follow their failure to understand His message (vv42–44). It's no wonder Jesus was weeping. They thought He was the mighty deliverer who could liberate them from Roman domination by leading a military uprising, they failed to realise that He had come to deliver them from so much more, from their sins.

Leader's Notes

Opening Icebreaker

Consider factors such as change, cost, doubt, fear and security. When God calls, we have the assurance that He is with us in any circumstance.

Aim of the Session

To show that we should seize every opportunity to use our gifts for God!

Discussion Starters

1. Without God's power it is impossible to achieve anything of lasting value. 'Unless the LORD builds the house, the builders labour in vain. Unless the LORD watches over the city, the guards stand watch in vain' (Psa. 127:1). This does not negate the importance of human response to God's call. All Christians are chosen by God to serve Him according to their various gifts and abilities (John 15:16; 1 Pet. 2:9). Think about what God's plan might be for your life.

2. Elisha's request to say goodbye to his parents was permissible because he was willing to follow Elijah without undue delay. He proved this by his actions (1 Kings 19:21). Conversely, the man with whom Jesus dealt with was half-hearted. Jesus is able to

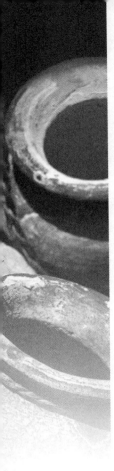

search hearts and to read minds (Mark 2:8). He detected that this man's desire to go home was not so that he could sever his connections, but rather to delay his commitment. Compare this man with Paul (Phil. 3:12–14) – and consider where you stand!

3. This relates back to this week's icebreaker. Some people do not accept God's call because they think its demands are too great. Jesus said to a wealthy man, 'Go, sell everything you have and give to the poor, and you will have treasure in heaven. Then come, follow me' (Mark 10:21). Jesus did not require this of all His wealthy followers but, in this instance, it was vital. The man obviously loved his goods more than his God. Commitment always involves a certain cost.

4. Elisha relinquished the status and privilege of his current position to become a servant. Peter, James and John left everything to follow Jesus (Luke 5:1–11). Levi resigned his post as a public tax collector in order to serve Jesus (Luke 5:27–28). These men did not hesitate for a moment to abandon their former way of life. God requires each of us to sacrifice what is necessary to fulfil the demands of our particular calling.

5. There are many notable examples of biblical perseverance (see Gen. 32:26; Num. 14:9; Job 13:15; 2 Cor. 4:1,16). Elisha persevered no matter how things appeared outwardly (2 Kings 2:1–6). God gives His people the strength to persevere when they are discouraged (Heb. 12:1–3).

6. Good leaders are people who are focused on what they can do for God and other people. Look at 1 Timothy 3:1–12 and Titus 1:6–9. In these verses, Paul lists many characteristics that should apply to anyone in church leadership.

7. The mother of James and John asked for places of great honour for her sons in God's future kingdom. Jesus told her that whoever wants to be great must be a servant, and whoever wants to be first must become a slave – just as the Son of Man came not to be served but to serve others, and to give his life as a ransom for many (Matt. 20:20–28). Jesus emphasized the need for service and sacrifice for the sake of others. This is the norm for the lives of His followers.

8. 'Self-praise is no honour,' says a proverb. This is especially applicable to spiritual things. 'For all those who exalt themselves will be humbled, and those who humble themselves will be exalted' (Luke 14:11). A willingness to serve one another is God's standard for true greatness and such people will be blessed. God acknowledges the prayers of the humble (Dan. 10:12).

Week 2: Where is the Lord, the God of Elijah?

Opening Icebreaker

Consider practical disciplines such as adequate rest, a healthy diet, exercise and a balance between work, ministry and family time. Spiritual disciplines include prayer and familiarity with God's Word.

Aim of the Session

To remind ourselves that an understanding of God's continual presence, power and provision can enable us to achieve much more than we could ask or hope.

Discussion Starters

1. Christians can be likened to people who hand over the baton in a relay race. Paul said, 'I consider my life worth nothing to me; my only aim is to finish the race and complete the task the Lord Jesus has given me' (Acts 20:24). Later he could say, 'I have finished the race' (2 Tim. 4:7). His concern now is for the younger generation whose responsibility it would be to guard the truth of God's Word and pass it on. God changes His workers, but His work continues.

2. People are wise to study history because the past provides lessons for the present and guidance for the future. However, it is unhealthy to dwell in the past because God does something new in every generation. There is no time like the present. To be unduly worried about past failures or totally satisfied with past successes will arrest future progress.

3. Elisha wanted God to do for him what He had previously done for Elijah. Turning back to the River Jordan, Elisha repeated the miracle of dividing the water. This was a sign that his request had been granted. The same Spirit controlling Elijah, was Elisha's also. Elijah's cloak that had fallen from him when he went up to heaven was the earthly symbol of the spiritual power now possessed by Elisha. He would start where Elijah finished.

4. The prophets from Jericho saw Elisha strike the water with the cloak that had fallen from Elijah. Then the river divided, and Elisha went across on dry ground. This action confirmed to them that Elisha 'possessed the spirit of Elijah' and should therefore be acknowledged as their leader (2 Kings 2:15).

5. Elisha is obviously the new leader. Yet the prophets react by saying, 'Can we go and search for Elijah?' It was important to them to try and ascertain what had happened to him. Maybe God had simply taken him elsewhere? Elijah had been known to disappear and then reappear (1 Kings 18:12).

6. It is unlikely that the prophets witnessed the actual ascension of Elijah; that appears to have been only seen by Elisha. He knew that Elijah had gone to be with the Lord and that they could not have him back. Any search for him would be futile and Elisha did not want to encourage the prophets to live in the past, so he tells them to not look for him.

7. Elisha stressed that the prophets should not search for Elijah, but they kept urging him until he was embarrassed. Therefore, Elisha dealt with them as a wise father deals with stubborn children – letting them have their own way, to a point, so as to learn from the hard school of experience. Following their fruitless search, he did not rebuke them but simply said, 'Didn't I tell you not to go?' (2 Kings 2:18). Elisha's leadership was now firmly established and he could proceed with the work to which God had called him.

8. Elijah and Elisha exercised a faith that could use the supernatural power of God. That same power is available to us today. A little faith in an omnipotent God will make things that are utterly beyond human capability possible. We have to make ourselves wholly available to God's leading (John 15:5).

Week 3: Miracles

Opening Icebreaker

Consider factors such as your own inadequacies, the unreasonable demands of society, unfair criticism and being let down. It is an encouragement to know that God is always with you wherever you are (Josh. 1:9).

Aim of the Session

To show that the miracles of Elisha revealed the greatness of God to people in need.

Discussion Starters

1. God does not perform miracles to amaze people or to satisfy their curiosity. Miracles are signs that point to something or someone. Elisha revealed the almighty power and love of his God by reviving a widow's dead son (2 Kings 4:8–37). Jesus said, 'The works I do in my Father's name testify about me' (John 10:25). The words and works of Jesus substantiate the claim that He is the Messiah.

2. Miracles, signs and wonders may be performed by pagan priests, magicians and others (Exod. 7:8–12). Many will say on Judgment Day that they have performed miracles in Jesus' name and He will tell them plainly, 'I never knew you. Away from me, you evildoers!' (Matt. 7:22–23). Such people are deceived and used by Satan to deceive others. They cannot, however, deceive Jesus, the Judge and Lord before whom they will finally appear.

3. The throwing of the salt into the spring prophesied that God would purify the polluted state of people's hearts and lives through using a new vessel and salt, a cleansing agent, into that condition. Jericho was cursed (Josh. 6:26), and we are under the curse of the law (Gal. 3:10). Hence, Christ's death upon the cross was essential for cleansing our lives. John 4:13–14 compares physical water to the living water which Jesus bestows.

4. Elisha accompanied Elijah all the way and thus received the double portion of his anointing – God's best for his life (2 Kings 2:1–14). At what stage of the journey do we stop? By having faithfulness in little things, Elisha displayed evidence of being fit for greater responsibilities. Heavenly rewards await those who are faithful in their stewardship (Luke 19:17; Rev. 2:10).

5. Both women showed hospitality to God's servants. Even so, they experienced desperate need and were about to lose their children: one through death, and the other through slavery. Directed by the ministry of the two prophets, they faithfully made use of their meagre resources. As a result, God intervened and they were amply provided for. Let us come to Him with receptive hearts and discover that Christ's grace is restricted only by our ability to receive.

6. God gave us the ultimate gift in His Son (John 3:16). Therefore, we can surely trust Him for all we need to live life for His glory (Matt. 6:31–33; Phil. 4:19; 2 Pet. 1:3–4).

7. The miracle of the floating axe head was not only a demonstration of God's almighty power, but also of the infinite provision for His people. Our problems are important to God, even the very little ones. What a privilege it is to carry everything to God in prayer (Phil. 4:6–7).

8. Probably many unusual events today are misinterpreted as miracles. Nevertheless, because God is the same God, a miracle is no less likely to occur today than it did in the past, unless it can be established that He no longer does such things. That, however, would deny numerous personal statements of apparently reliable witnesses. Could all these people be deluded? Or is it more likely that God still intervenes supernaturally in nature and human affairs when He has a reason to do so? Surely, what is impossible from a human perspective is possible for our all-powerful Creator God!

Week 4: Miraculous Healing

Opening Icebreaker

To spark ideas amongst the group, read Habakkuk 3:17–18 and Philippians 4:4–13. Lasting happiness is dependent on the certainty of heaven, where we will be liberated from the trials and troubles of our present life.

Aim of the Session

To consider what the Bible says about God's healing power and its relevance for today.

Discussion Starters

1. The Israelite girl was concerned about Naaman whereas the king thought only of himself and his kingdom. She had confidence in God and that His prophet Elisha would be able to heal Naaman's leprosy. The king of Israel did not know where to turn for an answer

and panicked (2 Kings 5:7). The girl, unlike the king, demonstrated a genuine faith in God and a genuine love for her neighbour (Matt. 22:34–40).

2. The reception given to Naaman by Elisha was not what he had expected. He had come to the prophet's door with his own plan of how he would be cured. He expected Elisha to greet him personally and he was further insulted by being told by a messenger to go and wash himself seven times in the River Jordan. Naaman was angry with God's man, God's message and God's method. But as he was leaving, his servants persuaded him to humbly receive healing by washing himself. What a privilege it is to have those around us who will tell us our faults in a constructive way.

3. Elisha's refusal to accept Naaman's gifts is especially notable since the event is set in a time of famine (2 Kings 4:38; 7:1–20). The testimony of Naaman would be that God had taken nothing from him but his leprosy.

4. Naaman showed a degree of superstition here, but his intention was good. Even so, it reveals that imperfections can often be mixed with true faith. Naaman's understanding of God was weak.

5. It was impossible to love the God of Israel and bow to Rimmon at the same time. Naaman's work, however, brought him into Rimmon's presence. Thus he would go through the motions and bow down in body, but not in spirit. It appears that Elisha was not too concerned about this compromise. He probably knew that God who had cured Naaman of his leprosy would have no difficulty in eventually purging his heart. Sanctification is a gradual and progressive renewal of our heart, which results in a change of character.

6. Every unconverted sinner is a leper in a spiritual
    sense and it will result in death (Rom. 6:23).
    Only God's remedy for sin is sufficient (John 14:6).
    Initially Naaman's problem was pride, but like
    many people he finally surrendered his life to God.

7. Gehazi experienced the great privilege of being very
    close to a man of God, yet succumbed to the sin of
    covetousness. 'You cannot serve both God and Money'
    (Luke 16:13). He had a corrupt heart and failed to
    understand that though you can fool some people
    some of the time, you cannot ever fool God. There are
    numerous examples of this within the Bible, such as:
    Achan (Josh. 7); Ananias and Sapphira (Acts 5:1–10)
    and Judas Iscariot (Matt. 26:14–16, 20–21).

8. People in Old Testament times often believed that disaster
    and disease were punishments for sin (Job 4:7). Such
    reasoning was still common amongst the early followers
    of Jesus (John 9:2). Often, sin and sickness are closely
    associated in the Bible because God has pronounced just
    judgments upon the disobedient. Miriam (Num. 12) and
    Gehazi became leprous because of their sin. However, it
    does not always follow that an individual's suffering is due
    to their personal sin. The entire Book of Job reveals that
    suffering is not necessarily due to the sin of the sufferer.

Week 5: Divine Guidance

Opening Icebreaker

Consider the necessity of seeking God's will through prayer,
through studying the Bible, through the wise counsel of
others, and by discerning the circumstances around you.

Aim of the Session

To show that if God is with us there is no problem that cannot be conquered. If God is against us, we labour in vain.

Discussion Starters

1. Jehoshaphat, the king of Judah, was a godly man and God had honoured him (see 2 Chron. 17:3–9). The combined Israelite, Judean, and Edomite invasion against the rebel Moabites, however, was a foolish mistake. He should not have formed an alliance with wicked people.

2. As a Christian, it is important to try and avoid involvement with anything that undermines Christian values and our relationship with God. That is not to say that Christians should satisfy all of our recreational and social needs within the spiritual environment of the church. We benefit from close Christian fellowship, but let us also remember the necessity of being salt and light in the world (Matt. 5:13–16).

3. Jehoshaphat was blessed, despite having strayed from God. Furthermore, his unrighteous associates who despaired for their lives were also rescued. How often has a godly man or woman, by their prayers and presence, been a blessing to those who have rejected God? For example, a whole ship's company were rescued because Paul was among them (Acts 27:33–44).

4. When an appeal for help came from the king of Israel, Jehoshaphat did not wait to discern God's will in the matter. He foolishly joined forces with an ungodly ally; a venture that was certain to have serious repercussions (2 Kings 3:4–10). Prayer and knowledge of the Scriptures enable us to discern

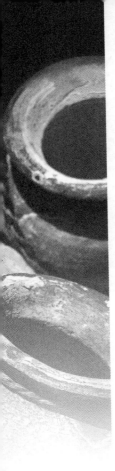

God's will. Consider Psalm 25:4–5; 2 Timothy 3:16–17; Proverbs 3:5–6 and James 1:5–8.

5. The king tore his robes in despair. People could see that he was wearing sackcloth next to his skin as an expression of repentance. This would appear to be a promising sign of his total dependence upon God, but his subsequent behaviour proved otherwise. The king in sackcloth vows to destroy God's prophet, Elisha. The king's anger then turned against the Lord Himself (2 Kings 6:33). What he did and what he said are clearly incompatible with true repentance.

6. In difficult situations, people will often find someone to blame. Why the king of Israel's anger was directed towards Elisha is not clear. Most likely it was because of Elisha's mercy to the soldiers from Aram (see 2 Kings 6:21–23). It would appear to the king that this was the cause of the present troubles. Furthermore, the king may also have believed that Elisha was failing to intercede with God for the relief of the siege.

7. The lepers were facing death from either starvation or leprosy. Their only hope was to plead for mercy. They step out in faith and experience a provision far greater than anything they could have imagined. So it is for all sinners who come to Christ. The lepers soon realised that what had been provided was not just for them. Accordingly, all Christians have a duty to tell others that God saves people through the work of Christ.

8. The prophecy of judgment (2 Kings 7:2), as well as that of provision (v16) were exactly fulfilled. God always meets the needs of His people when they trust Him. Unbelief, however, forfeits blessing and ultimately leads to God's judgment and punishment. If the officer had listened to God's prophet, then things would have been very different. Jesus Christ is God's provision for us (John 6:35; 8:12; 10:9–10 and 11:25–26).

Week 6: Divine Protection

Opening Icebreaker

God's ultimate goal for each one of us is that we learn how to first love Him and then others. Love is the only force capable of transforming an enemy into a true friend.

Aim of the Session

To emphasize the fact that God is our personal protector.

Discussion Starters

1. The hostility shown to Elisha was not that of mischievous youths but something far more serious. It was a premeditated attempt to discredit him and a challenge to the supernatural power of the God he served. God cannot be mocked. A man reaps what he sows (Gal. 6:7).

2. Bethel, the 'house of God', had once been one of the most sacred places in the land of Israel. By the time of Jeroboam, however, it had become a stronghold of a false religion (1 Kings 12:26–29) which rivalled the true religion of Israel. Bethel became Beth Aven, the 'house of wickedness' (Hosea 10:5). Godly people will always encounter opposition in wicked places.

3. All Christians should expect, at some time, to encounter opposition. Jesus said to His followers, shortly before His death, that they will be hated and persecuted because of Him (Matt. 10:22; John 15:20). Paul reminded Timothy that, 'In fact, everyone who wants to live a godly life in Christ Jesus will be persecuted' (2 Tim. 3:12). This is a truth that Scripture repeatedly proclaims. Christians will be social misfits in a sinful world and so it follows that persecution is inevitable.

4. No matter what we experience, God is there to encourage and lead us (Rom. 8:38–39; 2 Cor. 1:3–5). Jesus was without sin, and yet He was insulted; but He accepted the insults with love in order to bring people back to God (1 Peter 2:21–23). He, who suffered for us, is our example. It is a mistake to fight fire with fire or anger with anger because it will only inflame a situation. The solution of the world's problems lays in the power of love, not the love of power.

5. Paul's testimony is that Christ's grace is sufficient for him (Phil. 4:12–13). That is why he was able to face challenges such as pain, insults and persecution (2 Cor. 12:10). God does not necessarily remove our problems, but He does enable us to conquer them. Many of God's people have discovered that where the Holy Spirit intervenes there is no problem that is too great. Consider Zechariah 4:6; 1 Samuel 16:13 and Acts 4:31. In contrast, those who dwell only on the present problems will encounter difficulty and failure.

6. Good works are to be expected of a Christian; though, by themselves, these acts do not earn salvation (Eph. 2:8–10). God will treat people according to how they treat His servants and ultimately to the way in which they treat Jesus (Matt. 25:31–46).

7. Angels play a prominent role in protecting and guiding God's people. This is evident in the life of Elisha (2 Kings 6:15–17). An angel went before Abraham's servant in finding a wife for Isaac (Gen. 24:7, 40). Paul received assurance from an angel that no lives would be lost (Acts 27:23–26). An angel directed Philip so that he could meet an Ethiopian eunuch and lead him to Christ (Acts 8:26). Angels supported Jesus during His ministry on earth (Matt. 4:11; Luke 22:43). Had Jesus wanted, He could have received the help of more than twelve legions of angels (Matt. 26:53).

8. Numerous stories are told by people of how God sent His angels to help them. Is it possible that they are all figments of their imagination? No, we must accept that angels intervene in human affairs today because of what God says (Psa. 91:11). God's Word is absolutely final.

Week 7: A Ministry Fulfilled

Opening Icebreaker

Consider the importance of getting to know God intimately through studying the Bible (Psa. 119:105), the importance of prayer (James 1:5) and seeking the counsel of others (Prov. 12:15).

Aim of the Session

To show that restoration is the experience of the righteous, and retribution is the experience of the unrighteous.

Discussion Starters

1. Gehazi went from Elisha's presence and he was leprous; his skin was as white as snow (2 Kings 5:27). When he next appears upon the scene (2 Kings 8:4), there is no mention of his leprosy. It is possible, though unlikely, that the king would talk with someone who had a contagious disease. Does this suggest that Gehazi had repented and found restoration? The Bible does not tell us and so it is impossible to give a definite answer to this question, but fortunately God is all knowing and so we can rest in this knowledge.

2. This incident shows how abundantly God provides for His people. The woman from Shunem had been good to Elisha and for the sake of the kingdom of God, had willingly sacrificed time and money (2 Kings 4:8–10). God would now help her because she had learned to trust Him. God has promised to abundantly bless obedience (2 Kings 7:1; Mal. 3:10).

3. 2 Kings 1:2 tells us that Ahaziah, the king of Israel, consulted Baal-Zebub, the god of Ekron, to see if he will recover from his illness. In contrast, Ben-Hadad, the pagan king of Aram, consulted the God of Israel to see if he will recover. He realised that his own gods were of no use to him in this desperate situation and therefore he turns to the Lord and His prophet. Many people turn to God in a time of crisis.

4. Hazael had been promised that he would be king but, because of impatience, he murdered Ben-Hadad. God knew everything that he would do. Every person's secrets are known to God. Such awareness that God knows everything should influence the way that we live. Another lesson is that one wrong step will often lead to another. Hazael, step by step, did all the dreadful things, just as God had said.

5. Consider Numbers 14:43; 2 Kings 17:1–6 and 2 Chronicles 36:15–17. The betrayal of Jesus by Judas was necessary for the scriptures to be fulfilled (Acts 1:16).

6. Elisha gets Jehoash to symbolically defeat the enemy. Jehoash does so but the extent of victory is limited because he showed a lack of zeal for God (2 Kings 13:19). No wonder Elisha was angry with him. Do we go so far, but not all the way in our walk with God?

7. When Elisha died there appeared to be no one to carry on his work. God, however, was still present and this miracle of a dead man being revived encouraged the people to still trust in Him. The lasting influence of true servants of God is never in vain; but when those who are dead speak to us through their works, we must be sure to give God all the glory. This incident also had a prophetic significance in that it points us to Christ's resurrection and the fact that He did not die for His own benefit but for the benefit of His people (Matt 27:50–53).

8. Elisha loved God more than anyone or anything else. As a result, he was willing to sacrifice for the good of others. He obeyed the two most important commandments (Matt. 22:37–40). He was energised by the Spirit that once empowered Elijah, and that Spirit can energise people today to effectively serve God. End this study by giving everyone in the group the opportunity to discuss any questions they may still have about Elisha's life.

Notes ...

Notes ...

Journey through the Bible as it happened in a year of daily readings

Read through the entire Bible in a year with 366 daily readings from the New International Version (NIV) arranged in chronological order.

Beautiful charts, maps, illustrations and diagrams make the biblical background vivid, timelines enable you to track your progress, and a daily commentary helps you to apply what you read to your life.

A special website also provides character studies, insightful articles, photos of archaeological sites and much more for increased understanding and insight.

Cover to Cover Complete – NIV Edition
1,600 pages, hardback with ribbon marker, 140x215mm
ISBN: 978-1-85345-804-0

smallGroup central

*All of our small group ideas
and resources in one place*

Online:

www.smallgroupcentral.org.uk
is filled with free video teaching,
tools, articles and a whole host
of ideas.

On the road:

A range of seminars themed for
small groups can be brought to
your local community. Contact us at
hello@smallgroupcentral.org.uk

In print:

Books, study guides and DVDs
covering an extensive list of themes,
Bible books and life issues.

Log on and find out more at:
www.smallgroupcentral.org.uk

Latest resource

The Beatitudes – Immersed in the grace of Christ
by John Houghton

The eight Beatitudes, or blessings, mark the approach road to Jesus' groundbreaking Sermon on the Mount. They are among His best known but least understood words.

This study guide unearths meaning from the Beatitudes. There's as much to be said for us today as there was all those centuries ago about the needy, the sad, the powerless, the cheated, the carers, the purists and the blamed, for all of us.

72-page booklet, 210x148mm
ISBN: 978-1-78259-495-6

The bestselling *Cover to Cover* Bible Study Series

1 Corinthians
Growing a Spirit-filled church
ISBN: 978-1-85345-374-8

2 Corinthians
Restoring harmony
ISBN: 978-1-85345-551-3

1 Peter
Good reasons for hope
ISBN: 978-1-78259-088-0

2 Peter
Living in the light of God's promises
ISBN: 978-1-78259-403-1

1 Timothy
*Healthy churches –
effective Christians*
ISBN: 978-1-85345-291-8

23rd Psalm
The Lord is my shepherd
ISBN: 978-1-85345-449-3

2 Timothy and Titus
Vital Christianity
ISBN: 978-1-85345-338-0

Abraham
Adventures of faith
ISBN: 978-1-78259-089-7

Acts 1–12
Church on the move
ISBN: 978-1-85345-574-2

Acts 13–28
To the ends of the earth
ISBN: 978-1-85345-592-6

Barnabas
Son of encouragement
ISBN: 978-1-85345-911-5

Bible Genres
Hearing what the Bible really says
ISBN: 978-1-85345-987-0

Daniel
Living boldly for God
ISBN: 978-1-85345-986-3

David
A man after God's own heart
ISBN: 978-1-78259-444-4

Ecclesiastes
*Hard questions and
spiritual answers*
ISBN: 978-1-85345-371-7

Elijah
A man and his God
ISBN: 978-1-85345-575-9

Elisha
A lesson in faithfulness
ISBN: 978-1-78259-494-9

Ephesians
Claiming your inheritance
ISBN: 978-1-85345-229-1

Esther
For such a time as this
ISBN: 978-1-85345-511-7

Fruit of the Spirit
Growing more like Jesus
ISBN: 978-1-85345-375-5

Galatians
Freedom in Christ
ISBN: 978-1-85345-648-0

God's Rescue Plan
*Finding God's fingerprints
on human history*
ISBN: 978-1-85345-294-9

Great Prayers of the Bible
Applying them to our lives today
ISBN: 978-1-85345-253-6

Hebrews
Jesus – simply the best
ISBN: 978-1-85345-337-3

Hosea
The love that never fails
ISBN: 978-1-85345-290-1

Isaiah 1–39
Prophet to the nations
ISBN: 978-1-85345-510-0

Isaiah 40–66
Prophet of restoration
ISBN: 978-1-85345-550-6

James
Faith in action
ISBN: 978-1-85345-293-2

Jeremiah
The passionate prophet
ISBN: 978-1-85345-372-4

John's Gospel
Exploring the seven miraculous signs
ISBN: 978-1-85345-295-6

Joseph
The power of forgiveness and reconciliation
ISBN: 978-1-85345-252-9

Judges 1–8
The spiral of faith
ISBN: 978-1-85345-681-7

Judges 9–21
Learning to live God's way
ISBN: 978-1-85345-910-8

Luke
A prescription for living
ISBN: 978-1-78259-270-9

Mark
Life as it is meant to be lived
ISBN: 978-1-85345-233-8

Mary
The mother of Jesus
ISBN: 978-1-78259-402-4

Moses
Face to face with God
ISBN: 978-1-85345-336-6

Names of God
Exploring the depths of God's character
ISBN: 978-1-85345-680-0

Nehemiah
Principles for life
ISBN: 978-1-85345-335-9

Parables
Communicating God on earth
ISBN: 978-1-85345-340-3

Philemon
From slavery to freedom
ISBN: 978-1-85345-453-0

Philippians
Living for the sake of the gospel
ISBN: 978-1-85345-421-9

Prayers of Jesus
Hearing His heartbeat
ISBN: 978-1-85345-647-3

Proverbs
Living a life of wisdom
ISBN: 978-1-85345-373-1

Revelation 1–3
Christ's call to the Church
ISBN: 978-1-85345-461-5

Revelation 4–22
The Lamb wins! Christ's final victory
ISBN: 978-1-85345-411-0

Rivers of Justice
Responding to God's call to righteousness today
ISBN: 978-1-85345-339-7

Ruth
Loving kindness in action
ISBN: 978-1-85345-231-4

The Beatitudes
Immersed in the grace of Christ
ISBN: 978-1-78259-495-6

The Covenants
God's promises and their relevance today
ISBN: 978-1-85345-255-0

The Creed
Belief in action
ISBN: 978-1-78259-202-0

The Divine Blueprint
God's extraordinary power in ordinary lives
ISBN: 978-1-85345-292-5

The Holy Spirit
Understanding and experiencing Him
ISBN: 978-1-85345-254-3

The Image of God
His attributes and character
ISBN: 978-1-85345-228-4

The Kingdom
Studies from Matthew's Gospel
ISBN: 978-1-85345-251-2

The Letter to the Romans
Good news for everyone
ISBN: 978-1-85345-250-5

The Lord's Prayer
Praying Jesus' way
ISBN: 978-1-85345-460-8

The Prodigal Son
Amazing grace
ISBN: 978-1-85345-412-7

The Second Coming
Living in the light of Jesus' return
ISBN: 978-1-85345-422-6

The Sermon on the Mount
Life within the new covenant
ISBN: 978-1-85345-370-0

Thessalonians
Building Church in changing times
ISBN: 978-1-78259-443-7

The Ten Commandments
Living God's Way
ISBN: 978-1-85345-593-3

The Uniqueness of our Faith
What makes Christianity distinctive?
ISBN: 978-1-85345-232-1

Courses and events

Waverley Abbey College

Publishing and media

Conference facilities

Transforming lives

CWR's vision is to enable people to experience personal transformation through applying God's Word to their lives and relationships.

Our Bible-based training and resources help people around the world to:
• Grow in their walk with God
• Understand and apply Scripture to their lives
• Resource themselves and their church
• Develop pastoral care and counselling skills
• Train for leadership
• Strengthen relationships, marriage and family life and much more.

Our insightful writers provide daily Bible-reading notes and other resources for all ages, and our experienced course designers and presenters have gained an international reputation for excellence and effectiveness.

CWR's Training and Conference Centres in Surrey and East Sussex, England, provide excellent facilities in idyllic settings – ideal for both learning and spiritual refreshment.

 CWR Applying God's Word
to everyday life and relationships

CWR, Waverley Abbey House,
Waverley Lane, Farnham,
Surrey GU9 8EP, UK

Telephone: **+44 (0)1252 784700**
Email: **info@cwr.org.uk**
Website: **www.cwr.org.uk**

Registered Charity No. 294387
Company Registration No. 1990308